Y0-CRB-103

The Three Branches of Government

Working as a Team

Emma Carlson Berne

COMPUTER SCIENCE For the REAL World™

Rosen Classroom™

Published in 2018 by The Rosen Publishing Group, Inc.
29 East 21st Street, New York, NY 10010

Book Design: Jennifer Ryder-Talbot
Editor: Caitie McAneney

Photo Credits: Cover Orhan Cam/Shutterstock.com; p. 6-7 Drop of Light/
Shutterstock.com; p. 9 Cvandyke/Shutterstock.com; p. 10-11 turtix/
Shutterstock.com; p. 12 Steven Frame/Shutterstock.com; p. 15 Everett Historical/
Shutterstock.com; p. 16-17 Keith Tarrier/Shutterstock.com; p. 19 National Archive/
Newsmakers/Getty Images; p. 20-21 https://commons.wikimedia.org/wiki/File:Supreme_
Court_of_the_United_States_-_Roberts_Court_2017.jpg.

Library of Congress Cataloging-in-Publication Data
Names: Berne, Emma Carlson.
Title: The three branches of government: working as a team / Emma Carlson Berne.
Description: New York : Rosen Classroom, 2018. | Series: Computer Kids: Powered by
Computational Thinking | Includes glossary and index.
Identifiers: LCCN ISBN 9781538353066 (pbk.) | ISBN 9781538324363 (library bound) |
ISBN 9781538355596 (6 pack) | ISBN 9781508137313 (ebook)
Subjects: LCSH: United States--Politics and government--Juvenile literature.
Classification: LCC JK40.B47 2018 | DDC 320.473'04--dc23

Manufactured in the United States of America

CPSIA Compliance Information: Batch #WS18RC: For Further Information contact Rosen Publishing, New York, New York at 1-800-237-9932

Table of Contents

One Government, Three Branches

How does one government run a whole country? The United States is a democratic republic. That means the people get to elect representatives to make decisions for the country. There are three branches in the government. This makes sure that one group or person doesn't have too much power. The three branches have to work together to make positive change.

The U.S. federal government is one team split into legislative, executive, and judicial branches. The legislative branch is Congress, and it makes the laws. The executive branch is led by the president, who has the power to carry out laws. The judicial branch includes the Supreme Court, which has the power to **evaluate** laws and decide if they obey the **Constitution**.

Unites States Government

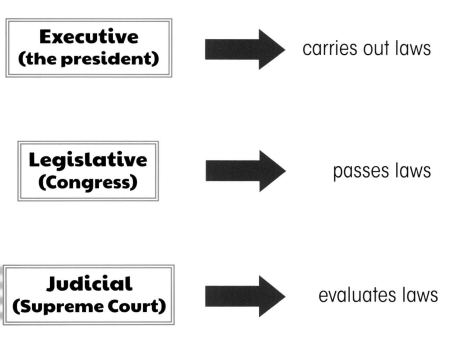

**Executive
(the president)** ➡ carries out laws

**Legislative
(Congress)** ➡ passes laws

**Judicial
(Supreme Court)** ➡ evaluates laws

The federal government is made up of three branches.
They have to work together as one team.

Checks and Balances

The makers of the U.S. Constitution set up the three-branch government for a reason. The three branches of government work together as a team and keep each other from gaining too much power. This is called a system of checks and balances. Each branch can support the other two branches or hold the other two branches back.

The U.S. government has a built-in system of checks and balances to make sure no one branch gets too powerful. Many people have to work together.

For example, the president—representing the executive branch—can **veto** or reject laws that Congress passes. Congress can **override** the president's veto. Congress can decide on members the president **appoints** to the **Cabinet**. Congress can even take away the president's job in serious situations. The Supreme Court can decide that laws passed by Congress and signed by the president are unconstitutional, or do not obey the Constitution.

The People's Congress

Congress is made up of the Senate and the House of Representatives. It is often the people's most direct line to government. This is because senators and representatives represent states and smaller areas. Everyone in America has two senators and a congressperson to speak for their area in Congress.

Congress can check the president in various ways. It can override a president's veto, saying, "We don't agree with your disagreement—we're passing this law!" Congress has the power to either approve or turn down people for the president's Cabinet. Congress can also **impeach** the president. This only happens in very serious cases—such as the president committing a crime.

U.S. Capitol

This is the U.S. Capitol, where senators and representatives meet to work on legislation, or laws.

The President's Job

The president is the head of the executive branch of government. He or she is also our nation's leader. The president acts as a **spokesperson** for the country. They make speeches when disasters strike an area or something bad happens. The president receives laws that Congress has passed. He or she can decide to sign the laws and carry them out, or they can decide to veto the laws.

White House

About four million other people work in the executive branch—everyone from members of the military to mail carriers to the secretary of the treasury. The president and vice president also work with their Cabinet. People in the Cabinet are called "secretaries," and they advise the president in different areas.

The president, vice president, and Cabinet members work to carry out laws that Congress passes.

The government allows for the branches to disagree at many different points. Disagreement often leads to positive growth when the branches work together to reach a **compromise**.

The Supreme Court

The Supreme Court's name describes who they are—the highest court in the nation. They have the last word on what is constitutional or unconstitutional. The Supreme Court and other federal courts make up the judicial branch. Lawyers bring cases to the Supreme Court when they think a law is unfair and unconstitutional. Supreme Court justices will listen, ask questions, and then decide to keep the law or change it.

The Supreme Court can remove the laws that Congress passed and the president signed. However, Supreme Court justices are first **nominated** by the president and are given final approval by Congress. That system makes sure that the president and Congress agree on a judge before giving them a job.

The War Powers Act

In 1973, the American people had a chance to see the system of checks and balances in action. Congress passed the War Powers Resolution of 1973, also called the War Powers Act.

Congress felt this act was necessary. From the 1950s through 1970s, the United States fought wars in Korea and Vietnam. These wars were brutal, bloody, and highly **controversial**. They were both fought without official **declarations** of war. The president in 1973 was Richard Nixon. He also ordered secret bombing attacks in Cambodia without telling Congress or the American people. Congress decided that it was time to limit the ability of the president to wage war on his own.

Many people thought the United States should not be fighting in Vietnam.

15

The Power to Wage War

When it comes to war, Congress and the president have to work together. The president is the head of the armed forces and is called the Commander in Chief. Congress has the power to declare war and provide the money and support for the war and troops.

The War Powers Act was passed after President Nixon order secret bombing raids.

Since it's the role of Congress to officially declare war, it should have had a good deal of control over when and where the United States fought. However, since the 1950s, presidents had been waging wars and fighting without officially declaring war. After twenty years of controversial fighting, Congress decided that the president's powers had to be checked. They needed to work together for the good of the American people.

Checks and Balances at Work

Because of the system of checks and balances, Congress could pass an act to limit the president's power. The Senate and the House of Representatives worked together to pass the War Powers Act of 1973. It stated that a president could not wage war without an official declaration of war.

President Nixon used his power to veto the resolution. He didn't want his powers limited. Congress fired back. They took a vote and overrode the veto. The resolution stood and the president's powers were limited. It may seem like the executive and legislative branches weren't working together in this case. However, the system of checks and balances served to protect and represent the American people.

Congress limited President Richard Nixon's ability to wage war.

The Court Weighs In

The Supreme Court has also been involved with the War Powers Act. In the 1983 case called *Immigration and Naturalization Services v. Chadha,* the Supreme Court decided that the type of control Congress used in the War Powers Act to limit the president was unconstitutional. This type of control is called a "legislative veto" and is used to give Congress more power over the president's decisions.

The Supreme Court's decision gave Congress less authority and the president more authority. Congress was checked under the system of checks and balances. Therefore, the power that Congress had given itself with the passage of the War Powers Act was lessened and presidential power was increased.

These are the justices of the U.S. Supreme Court in 2017.

Working Together for Change

The War Powers Act stands today, but it is still debated. Some groups think that Congress has too much power, and others think the president has too much power. These kinds of arguments are the very base of our government.

The three branches of our federal government are constantly pushing and pulling each other. It may seem as if checks and balances keep the branches from working together, but they actually work together every day. They make, pass, and evaluate laws that affect the American people. They use their skills and powers to make real change. By themselves, the branches can't get very much done. However, when they work together and compromise, we can see the U.S. government at its best.

Glossary

appoint: To name someone officially to a position.

Cabinet: A group of senior officials appointed by the president as special advisors.

compromise: A settlement of differences.

constitution: The basic laws by which a country or state is governed.

controversial: Causing arguments.

declaration: A document or speech that makes something formally or officially known.

evaluate: To determine the condition of something.

impeach: To charge with misconduct in office.

nominate: To suggest someone for an honor or job.

override: To take power away from something or someone.

spokesperson: A person who speaks for another or for a group.

veto: The exercise of the power of one branch of government to keep another branch from carrying out an act.

Index

A
appoint, 7

C
Cabinet, 7, 8, 11
compromise, 12, 22
Congress, 4, 5, 7, 8, 10, 11, 13, 14, 16, 17, 18, 19, 20, 21, 22
constitution, 4, 6, 7, 13
controversial, 14, 17

D
declaration, 14, 18

E
evaluate, 4, 5, 22
executive, 4, 5, 7, 10, 11, 18

I
impeach, 8

J
judicial, 4, 5, 13

L
legislative, 4, 5, 18, 20

N
Nixon, Richard, 14, 16, 18, 19
nominate, 13

O
override, 7, 8

P
president, 4, 5, 7, 8, 10, 11, 13, 14, 16, 17, 18, 19, 20, 21, 22

S
spokesperson, 10
Supreme Court, 4, 5, 7, 12, 13, 20, 21

V
veto, 7, 8, 10, 18, 20

W
War Powers Act, 14, 16, 18, 20, 21, 22